BROW LAMINATION

A GUIDE TO PERFECT

TABLE OF CONTENT

WHAT IS BROW LAMINATION

Brow lamination will give you fuller and thicker

eyebrows in as little as 45min

It will last up to 6-8 weeks, so you don't have to use much

brow make up.

This treatment is believed to be originated in Russia

We will be placing a solution on the eyebrows and

brushing them in an upwards direction for a fluffier look

or to the direction of the growth for more natural look.

It will correct curled eyebrows and make them look fuller.

For a fluffy look we can brush the eyebrows upwards, so

all of the hairs are facing the same direction.

Once they are set, we will be applying tinting lotion.

We will finish the treatment with a nourishing lotion.

It will not keep your eyebrows permanently brushed upwards and straight, but it will look/keep the hair in place for up to two months.

INTRODUCTION

Hello beautiful

Do you want to learn the art of brow lamination?

My name is Mirka. My passion is helping people start out on their own like I did many years ago in the beauty industry.

The following is a guide on how we/ourselves do this amazing treatment, it has helped many students, therapists and even clients understand the treatment in an easy to understand way.

Becoming a lash and brow artist has changed my life and that of many others.

We love everything lash, brow and tan.

See our full list of online courses at

www.beautytrainingonline.co.uk.

Our courses are held around the United Kingdom and

Slovakia, in classroom settings, online and 1-2-1. Our

Face2Face courses are fully accredited by ABT and our

online courses are approved by IICT and sold worldwide

once completed students gain our certificate which can

easily be printed and used.

ABOUT THE AUTHOR

A little bit about me that you may recognise in yourself!

I started working in a well-known department store in Windsor within fashion and beauty. This was always my passion.

Now I remember it like yesterday, I was 25 years old, it was a beautiful sunny day and I was stuck working indoors wishing I was outside.

Don't get me wrong I didn't hate my job I just wanted more from life.

My colleagues and customers were so lovely, but I wanted more! I wanted freedom!!!

Freedom to go outside, walk around the beautiful royal lakes that were nearby, grab a cocktail and sit outside of a pub with my friends and enjoy the sunshine, have that BBQ and chill in the garden and so on.

SEEING MY FRIENDS DOING WELL

A few of my friends had their own businesses and I have to admit I was a little jealous, but not in a bad way I just wished it was me!

They could work around their life not live life around their work, they would go on holidays whenever they wanted and buy that designer handbag I dreamed of.

I would constantly think "How long can I carry on like this" I was very confused but very afraid to start something new and take that leap.

Online I saw a girl posting about freelance work and talking about business with passion and how happy she is that she doesn't have a boss and a 9-5 job.

I knew instantly if she can do it, I will be able to do it too!!!

So, I quit my job because I knew I could do better, and the rest is a history…

I TOOK THE LEAP

Later I started my own salon in Windsor providing jobs to the local community and passing on my skills and knowledge.

Now I have beautiful twins who are at school, I'm working my hours around them and spending quality time with my family while still having a full-time income.

I am passing on my skills and knowledge to people of all ages and backgrounds because we love what we do.

I STARTED DOING BEAUTY SO CAN YOU!!!

I have been able to create the life I always wanted doing beauty and so can YOU! Part time hours on a full-time salary it's worth it!

Now we have taught many people to do it too. I am here to show you how you can have the life you have always wanted and deserved.

We hope you enjoy our guide on how to do the amazing and profitable Brow Lamination treatment.

Thank you again Mirka

Beauty By Mirka Part of Celo Tan & Lash

THE PATCH TEST

<u>BEFORE ANY TREATMENT YOU MUST DO A</u>

<u>PATCH TEST</u>

Patch testing is very important and is essential for every new client.

This must be carried out at least 48 hours before you start any treatment.

Clean the area first and:

- *Apply a little perming lotion on the micro brush and dab it behind your client's ear.*

- *Then repeat the above step with the fixing lotion.*

If there is any redness, itchiness or swelling do not carry out with the treatment.

As we go through hormonal changes throughout our lives our bodies sensitivity can change, so it is always better to patch test your client again after big life changes such as during pregnancy, after giving birth or if _you_ have changed your products…

And why do we have to do this?

By conducting a patch test you are protecting both your client (safety wise) and yourself.

The patch test is designed to ensure that your client is not allergic to any lotions or products that we are using.

Although it is unlikely that your client will experience an allergic reaction, it is always better to check.

The client's wellbeing should always be your highest priority.

For full information about Salon Health and Safety (COSHH) visit the government web site at the following link http://www.hse.gov.uk/coshh/index.htm

HYGIENE & SAFETY

BEFORE TREATMENT:

- Hair tied back, no jewellery, nails must be short, and tunic must be worn

- Client consultation form must be filled out signed and dated

- Explain the treatment to your client and any aftercare requirements

- Find out if client has had any reactions to a previous beauty treatment

- Make sure your client feels safe in your environment

- Ask your client to remove contact lenses before treatment (for comfort)

Stop the treatment if your client's brows become irritated

HYGIENE:

- Wash your hands thoroughly and use antibacterial gel before each client

- Line contact surfaces with disposable couch roll

- Never use the same micro brushes, mascara brushes or any disposable tools on different clients because of cross contamination

Sterilise equipment for a minimum of 20 minutes with Barbicide, 70% alcohol or in an autoclave

DURING AND AFTER THE TREATMENT:

- Clients eyes can be closed at all times during treatment
- Ensure there is appropriate ventilation and lighting
- Client must be comfortable during the treatment
- Do not forget to put nourishing lotion afterwards

TOOLS AND SUPPLIES

Before we start the treatment, we have to make sure we have all the tools that we need for brow lamination. These need to be ready and clean.

Tools we will need:

- Antibacterial gel (Always make sure your hands are clean with antibacterial gel before any contact with your client)

- Primer or OIL FREE makeup remover (Primer should be used on every client before we start doing the treatment. It is to remove extra oil or make up from the client's skin so the area we will work on is prepared for the treatment)

- Mascara brushes or brush (Brush eyebrows to the desired direction and shape)

- Adhesive (Only use one specialising in brow lamination. Must be water based. It is to stick eyebrows into the desired look)

- Perming lotion (solution that perm eyebrows into desire shape)

- Fixing lotion (to make new eyebrows more permanent)

- Nourishing lotion (condition and protects permed eyebrows)

- Microbrushes (used to applying perming, fixing and nourishing lotion)

www.eyeluvlashes.co.uk

- Cotton buds and cotton pads (to remove excess product)
- Water (clean the adhesive before applying tint)
- Different colours of tint (to tint client's eyebrows)
- Hydrogen peroxide 3% (to mix with your tinting lotion)
- Tinting brush (is to use to apply tint on the eyebrows)
- Tinting bowl (to mix hydrogen peroxide and tinting lotion together)
- Spatula, micro brush or orange stick (will help you to mark where to start, the highest point and where eyebrows should finish)
- White eyeliner (to make marks on the skin to help you to reach the desired look)

- Cling film (is to make the treatment more effective)

- Flannel (keep the warmth to speed up the process)

- Timer (to make sure you keep perming, fixing lotion and tinting lotion only for as long as said)

- Magnifying glasses and/or an extra light if necessary (It will help you to see eyebrows closer and use extra light in darker rooms where there is no natural daylight)

Example of light can be found here

Starter kit can be bought from Eyeluvlashes

Supplies:

As you will be doing brow lamination on a daily basis and doing more and more treatments you will find out which of the suppliers will have the best quality and prices.

Here are some places we order/ buy from:

Eyeluvlashes USE CODE 'CELO' AT CHECKOUT AND RECEIVE 10% OFF

Sally's

Ellison's (equipment, essentials)

You will over time find the best places to buy your equipment and products.

Please remember buying cheap isn't always a good idea for a number of reasons over time you will find great deals and suppliers which fit your needs

CLIENT CONSULTATION FORMS

Consultation forms give you an opportunity to gather all the information about your client.

Every client must fill out a consultation form.

Contraindications can be identified at this stage.

Explain that the procedure might take up to 45 minutes of them lying still.

You must explain to the client that the treatment is "semi-permanent"

Brow lamination will last for up to 6 – 8 weeks

Write down the look your clients are after for your future
reference

Keep clients record safe and in lockable cabinet for 7
years

Never share client's privacy with friends/ colleague.

If you are unsure if it is safe to proceed, refer the client to
their GP. Tell them to bring in a GP's consent form and
staple it to their consultation form this is for their
safety and your insurance.

Very important:

If you are in any doubt about client suitability for a

treatment, do NOT do the treatment

HAIR GROWTH

We have 3 stages of hair growth:

Anagen (Growth/ Active period) Phase

The anagen phase is also called the growth phase. This is
the phase when eyebrows are actively growing, and it
lasts between 30 and 45 days.

Catagen (Transition) Phase

The catagen phase is also known as the transition phase.
During this phase, the hair stops growing, and the hair
follicle shrink. This phase lasts between two and three
weeks.

Telogen (Resting) Phase

The telogen phase is also referred to as the resting phase. This phase can be 50- 100 days before the hair falls out and a new one begins to grow.

Our hair is growing from a root in the bottom of the follicle. The root is made up of cells of protein.

Blood from the blood vessels is feeding the root and makes the hair grow.

Hair is made up of 3 layers:

Cuticle – the outer layer. This is the protective layer of the hair shaft

Cortex – is beneath the cuticle. This is the main part of the hair. It has the colour pigments which make up the hair colour. Lots of fibre create a bundle and that gives extra strength for the hair. Keratin is formed in this layer.

Medulla – the middle of the hair. Not always present. This does not have any function.

HOW TO MEASURE THE CORRECT SHAPE OF THE EYEBROW

If you are working on the client's eyebrows, you can either provide them with a complete reshape or just maintenance of their current shape.

If you are maintaining their current shape you should just remove stray hairs and tidy the brows.

If you are providing the client with a reshape you will need to measure the brows and agree the shape with the client before you begin the treatment.

You will need to measure to see where the eyebrow should start and finish in order to create the perfect eyebrow shape for the client's face.

Take an orange stick from the outer corner of the nose up to the inner corner of the eye (pic - black line 1a) Any hairs which are on the nose side of this line will need to be removed (with client's permission) If you feel it will look "too bald" and want her eyebrows closer, you can place an orange stick on the top of her nostrils and imagine an invisible straight line can be seen on the following pages (pic - black line 1)

Take the orange stick from the outer corner of the nose up to the outer corner of the eye.

This is where the eyebrow should finish (with client's permission) (pic - black line 3)

You can measure where the highest arch of the brows should be by placing the orange stick over the clients slightly opened eye.

A diagonal line should go from the corner of the nose through the centre of the pupil. This will determine where the highest point of the arch should be (pic - black line 2)

You can also use the orange stick to measure across the top of the eye to see where the eyebrow should start and finish this will also allow you to see where the arch should be, and which area requires shaping.

Whilst you are measuring you should explain to the client where you are going to remove the hairs from and why so there are no surprises.

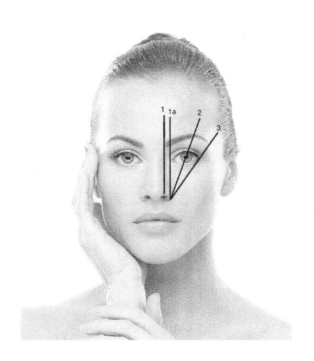

CONTRA-INDICATIONS & CONTRA-ACTIONS

Here are some examples of when not to proceed the treatment:

- Patch test reaction (redness, swelling and itchiness)

- Contact lenses must be removed prior to the procedure (for better comfort during threading/waxing and cleaning)

- Skin conditions around eye area such as eczema, psoriasis - Psoriasis is a long-lasting autoimmune disease which is characterised by patches of abnormal skin. These skin patches are typically red and itchy. Procedure will be very difficult to finish.

- Conjunctivitis - Is highly contagious. Not suitable for brow lamination. It is also known as pink eye, is inflammation of the outermost layer of the white part of the eye and the inner surface of the eyelid.

- Impetigo – Red skin that soon becomes a blister. It is highly contagious

- Ringworm – red rash on the skin looking like ring. It is highly contagious

- Styes - Is a small and painful lump on the eyelid. It can be inside or outside of the eyelid. It is actually an abscess filled with pus. It is usually caused by bacteria eye infection.

- Blepharitis - Blepharitis (/blɛfərˈaɪtɪs/ BLEF-ər-EYE-tis) is an eye condition characterized by chronic inflammation of the eyelid. Eyelid can be very itchy, irritated and red.

- Folliculitis – infection of a hair follicle. This is an acute inflammation which occurs with pus formation.

- Boils – it is a painful red bump on the skin caused by an infected hair follicle

- Scabies – skin is very itchy. It is a contagious skin condition.

A Contra - action is a reaction after treatment:

- Irritation or prickling

- Allergic reaction

In this situation immediately remove the product using damp cloth. If irritation does not cease, then advise the client to seek medical attention.

Do not proceed with treatment if you are unsure. Advise your client to seek medical help if you are unsure and tell them to bring a letter from their GP.

BROW LAMINATION STEP BY STEP

- Clean your hands thoroughly

- Use make up removal (oil free) to wipe client's eyebrows to get rid of natural oils and/or foundation

- Ask your client what they would like to achieve (fluffy brow, fuller look, straighten curly brow etc)

- Make the measurements (start of the brow, arch, end of the brow) and ask your client if she is happy with it)

- Make sure the eyebrows are dry from the cleaning product before you start

- Apply a thin coat of adhesive (specialised for the brow lamination treatment) onto your client's eyebrows. Do not use too much adhesive as it will create blockage and your product will not work that well on this area.

- Use disposable mascara brush or a Y brush to brush the eyebrows into the desired look.

- Brows must be tightly stuck on the skin (not loose). Apply adhesive in the inner corner and brush the eyebrows to the desired look. Then apply adhesive in the middle and stick the eyebrows into the desired look and then repeat it on the outer corner. If you section it like this, your adhesive will be always fresh, and you are using just a minimum glue as it is recommended.

- Ensure eyebrows are not overlapping, pointing the right direction (depends of what your client wants) no gaps and no curled ends. The way they will look now is the way they will look at the end.

Make sure the adhesive is dry before you move onto the next step.

- Now you can apply Lotion 1 with a dabbing motion onto the eyebrows making sure it is even by using micro-brush and leave it on for 8-10minutes (unless your lotion says otherwise) Please ask the manufacturer

  Very fine brow 8 min

  Fine or tinted brow 8 min

  Natural healthy brow 10 min

  Coarse healthy brow 10 min

- Timing is different from each supplier. Please follow their timing and instruction

- If your client would like fluffy look, you can apply the lotion on the roots only. Otherwise you can cover the whole hair. Do not leave lotion any longer than recommended as it could cause an over- process eyebrow (burn/frizz).

- Cover the eyebrows with the cling film and place the flannel over the eyebrows to preserve warmth (only if your manufacturers guidelines recommend this).

- Remove the Lotion 1 gently with dry cotton buds following the hair growth/direction

- Now you can apply Lotion 2 with a dabbing motion onto the eyebrows, evenly with a micro-brush and leave it on for 8-10 minutes (unless your lotion says otherwise).

  Please ask the manufacturer.

  Very fine, fine and tinted brows 8 minutes

  Natural healthy and course healthy brows 10 minutes

  Timing is different from each supplier. Please follow their timing and instruction

- If your client would like fluffy look, you can apply the lotion on the roots only. Otherwise you can cover the whole hair. Do not leave lotion any longer than recommended as it could cause an over- process eyebrow (burn/frizz).

- Cover the eyebrows with the cling film and place the flannel over the eyebrows to preserve warmth (if your manufacturers guidelines recommend this)

- Remove the Lotion 2 gently with dry cotton buds following the hair growth/direction

- Make sure your glue is properly removed from the hair. Use damp cotton pad/bud to remove excess glue if necessary.

- At this point you must hold tinting qualification

- Now you can apply tint on the eyebrows following the shape of your client's eyebrow (when using henna please double check with henna manufacturer as sometimes you might need to wait 24 hours before using henna)

- Remove tinting lotion with a damp cotton pad (not soaking wet)

- At this point you should hold a waxing or threading qualification (is advisable but not necessary) so you can tidy up your client's eyebrows.

- Online courses can be seen/purchased at www.beautytrainingonline.co.uk
  Write down in the consultation form what have you used on your client for your future reference (desired look, timing, tint colour etc)

IMPORTANT: Always preform brow shaping (waxing, threading, plucking) after the lamination and tinting. With all 3 methods (wax, thread and pluck) you are opening the pores.

ALWAYS follow the manufactures guidelines when using any product

- Then you can apply Lotion 3 to the entire brow with Microbrushes and leave it on to dry for 24 hours. Do not wash or remove.

- Explain aftercare to your client

PRODUCT ORDER

<u>PLEASE REMEMBER YOU MUST ONLY USE</u>

<u>PRODUCTS DESIGNED FOR</u>

<u>BROW LAMINATION</u>

Shape preparation with the white eyeliner

Adhesive is applied on the eyebrows

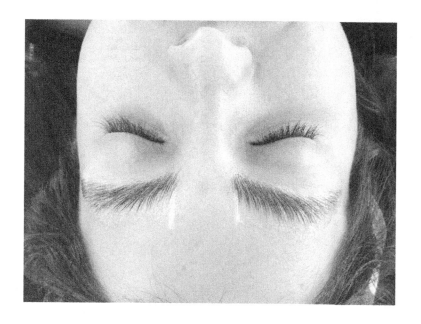

Lotion 1 is applied on the eyebrows

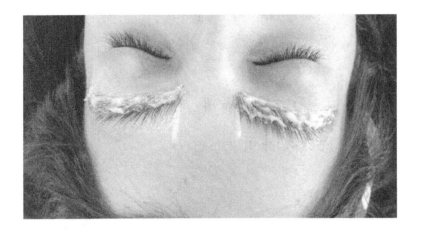

Cling film is placed on the eyebrows after we apply

Lotion 1 and Lotion 2 if this is what your manufacturers

guidelines require

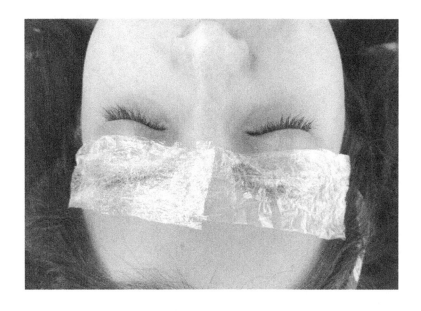

A flannel is used to cover the area to speed up the

process if recommended by manufacturer

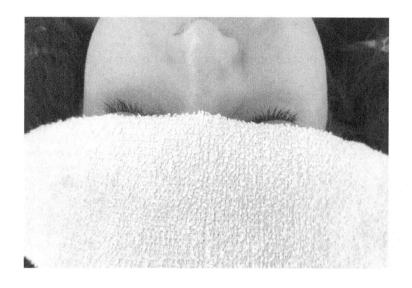

EYEBROW TINTING

- Use the correct colour for your client. Always use the products that are permitted for use in the EU or your state and meets with the cosmetic products (safety) regulations 1989 otherwise it will make your insurance invalid.

- Once you have chosen the colour you can now mix tint with hydrogen peroxide. Pea size of a tint would be used with 2-3 drops of hydrogen peroxide and mix it in the tint bowl with a plastic stick from your tinting lotion pack or with a brush. You will create a creamy consistency

- Apply the tint to the eyebrows. Start from the inner corner and work towards the outer corner evenly making sure all the brow hair is covered

- Repeat the process to the second eyebrow

- Keep the tint on according to the manufacturer's guidelines (3-5 minute) remember Eyebrow hair colour develops quicker than lash hair!

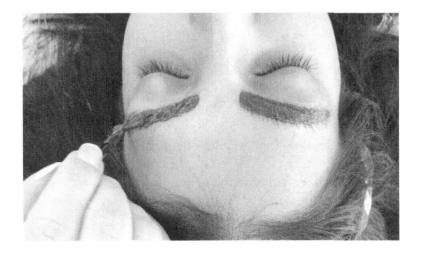

- Use a clean and dry cotton bud to wipe away any extra tint that may have gone off the desired shape of the brow

- Once the colour is developed use damp clean cotton pad to remove the tint. Place it on the eyebrow and wipe it across the eyebrow in an outward sweep

- Ensure that all tint is removed to prevent skin staining

- Use professional skin stain remover if you accidently stain client's skin

- Show the final look to your client making sure they are satisfied with the colour

- You can always re-apply the tint to the eyebrow if your clients desire a darker look

- Blonde hair develops colour rapidly if it is left for too long

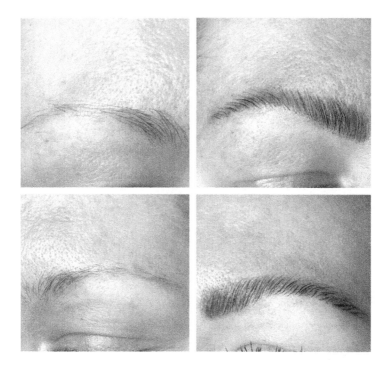

IMPORTANT

Never squeeze the product from the sachets/bottles close to your clients. Always squeeze it further away from their hair, clothes and face to avoid spillage.

AFTERCARE

Brow lamination aftercare:

1. Do not rub the brows at any stage

2. Do not get the eyebrows wet for the first 24 hours

3. Do not use sauna, steam room and avoid exercise that causes sweat for 24 hours

4. Do not pick or pull your eyebrows

5. Do not apply any oil based make up to the eyebrow area

6. Brow lamination will last up to 6-8weeks

BUSINESS SETUP

Business set up and Legal Requirements UK (at time of writing)

Legal requirements:

Client consultation before all beauty treatments is a legal requirement and failure to consult properly with clients before doing any treatment could invalidate your beauty therapy insurance. It is essential that you gather as much information from your clients about their medical history & allergies while checking for any contraindications keeping (securely) up to date records

<u>The insurance requirements for eyelash perm treatments</u>:

The minimum a salon should hold is employer's liability insurance as well as public liability insurance and professional indemnity insurance individuals will require a membership such as with ABT which can provide cover for approved courses and are great for mobile therapists.

The legal requirements for providing treatments to minors:

The age a client is at time of treatment may impact your insurance cover you must make sure that your insurance cover is valid for example some insurance providers state you need a signed consent form from a guardian or parent if the client is under 16 or 18 years old (depending on your location/country).

THINGS TO CONSIDER

Accounting:

It is very important to keep your books in order, so you know how much you are making, and spending remember income from any paid work is the taxable when you reach a certain threshold.

We started doing it ourselves but like us - as your business grows - you may need help as it can take up time you could conducting more treatments.

Tax:

Make sure you register as self-employed and/or declare your earnings if you are doing lashes as a side line nobody likes a tax dodger.

Business rates (if you are renting a premise or working from home):

You must look into business rates. If you are renting a salon or working from home this can also affect your home insurance and treatment cover. We started off mobile and believe this is a great way to begin your journeys!

Insurance & Membership:

Remember you must be trained and insured to offer treatments to customers

We are pleased to be able to recommend a wonderful company in the UK to students who do one of our online beauty courses for insurance needs. They provide extremely helpful cover and as our online courses are approved by IICT (approved in a number of countries) they will accept our certificates - once passing the course and case studies then insurance can be gained through them (conditions apply).

Data protection (record keeping):

You must always keep up to date records and make sure these (hard copies) are securely stored away.

Please also remember these are just guidelines it is up to the individual therapist to maintain all aspects of offering treatments and we hold no responsibility for your actions please remember regulations can change so please keep up to date records safe and secure.

MAXIMISING YOUR BUSINESS POTENTIAL

Find ways to stand out from your competition

You can lower your prices, offer a free treatment on a client's birthday, get one treatment and second half price, offer a loyalty card (every 10th visit for free), recommend to a friend and get 10% off and so on....

Know what you are learning

Never stop learning. Keep up to date with the newest treatments. People will ask you when there is something new on the market. Make sure you attend as many events as possible and you do your research on the internet about new techniques and looks.

Surround yourself with great people

When hiring someone you have to have that feeling they will be the one. Not only working with you in the team, but also, they must share your vision and be good at talking to the clients. More therapists = more clients.

Create a business plan

Where can you see yourself in 5 years' time? Write it down and leave it somewhere you can see it and work hard to reach your goals. Remember you can always gain confidence from failure.

<u>Very important - advertise as much as you can</u>

Try local newspaper, post flyers through the letter box, advertise in a local magazine, advertise in the windows of your local shops, keep a board outside your salon, create a Facebook page, keep Twitter or Instagram up-to-date and ask clients to tag you in it, leave your business cards in the restaurant where you visiting regularly (with owner's permission), volunteer a treatment in a prize draw, use LinkedIn, use YouTube, attend local networking events and build connections....

When doing mobile appointments remember to charge extra for your travel time and fuel. Some people charge £5 extra depending on how far they have to travel. We also ask that the client also pays a deposit plus provides us with parking as there is nothing worse than having to park miles away from your client's house TIME IS MONEY!

GDPR & YOU

General Data Protection Regulation

As of the 25th May 2018 all companies no matter how big or small must comply!

If you already are compliant with DPA then you will already understand part of GDPR but you must not mistake the two as being the same.

If you collect any data or information about your customers/clients and use it for marketing or share it with anyone then GDPR applies to you.

This includes any personal data about customers including name, address, telephone number, email address, date of birth and so on.

MARKETING TO CUSTOMERS

You must always have consent from each and every one of your clients to be able to send them any marketing.

Your messaging to your clients has to be clear and transparent and you must explain why you are collecting the data and what it is used for.

You must also record that the customer/client has given their consent

For example we have added links to all our sites which our clients have to agree they have read and agree too under the headings "T&C's & PRIVACY POLICY/STATEMENT" these agreements cover everything from….

What we collect

Why we collect it

How we use it

VERY IMPORTANTLY how a client/student can contact us to have their data removed in the future.

If you have existing clients you could update your customer records and ask them all to re-sign a consent form, you can add a box on the consent form specifically relating to marketing consent.

Please remember to always keep updated on new regulations and make sure you are actively applying them to your business practices it is your responsibility to check and follow all rules and regulations which apply to you as an individual.

THANK YOU AGAIN

Please remember this is a guide only - to offer these
treatments you must be insured and qualified along with
abide by your state, country and regions rules and
regulations we hold no reasonability for your actions

IF YOU WISH TO DO OUR ONLINE CERTIFICATED
COURSE PLEASE TAKE A LOOK AT OUR WEBSITE

www.beautytrainingonline.co.uk

DISCOUNT CODE

OUR FULL ONLINE COURSE INCLUDES VIDEO

TUTORIALS, ONGOING SUPPORT VIA EMAIL

TEXT AND SOCIAL MEDIA - PLUS OUR

CERTIFICATE ONCE PASSED

USE CODE "EBOOKCELO25" TO GET 25% OFF FOR

A LIMITED TIME

BEAUTY BY MIRKA

Mirka

Other online courses from us include

Russian Volume – Individual Lashes – Lash Lift – Spray

Tan – Nails – Waxing – Tinting – Threading & more

Made in the USA
Monee, IL
05 April 2025

15231314R00049